kindred knits

knitting for little ones near and far

by **Susan B. Anderson**

quince&co.

Published in 2017 by
Quince & Company, Inc
142 High Street
Suite 220
Portland, ME 04101

ISBN 978-0-9979187-2-4

Printed in the US

10

16

20

24

28

32

34

36

table of contents

Babies.

Hands down, nothing inspires people to knit more than the prospect of a new baby. I've known many a new mother, father, aunt, grandparent, or friend to take up knitting for the first time purely to welcome a new baby to the world. Knitting for a baby or toddler is a true gesture of love.

Kindred Knits is just this kind of gesture, a collection inspired by the little ones connected with us throughout our lives. The patterns are purposefully simple, so that all well wishes can be the point of concentration while creating, thus imbibing our hopes and dreams into the projects at hand.

The designs included in *Kindred Knits* cover many baby and toddler needs: A variety of simple sweater options, a blanket, a hat, a sweet ornament, and a doll or teddy bear sweater. My *String Along Toys*, also available through Quince & Co, complement this collection beautifully.

And for little ones far away, or for those wanting to knit a different size, I share a tutorial on how to create a sweater from scratch with only a few simple measurements taken from any size t-shirt, big or small.

Some information I've gathered through my own knitting and designing experience. And some of the information has been distilled from many other great top-down pattern writers who I would be remiss in not crediting: Barbara Walker, Ann Budd, and Wendy Bernard, to name a few. The easy step-by-step instructions will surely become a mainstay in your knitting library.

Kindred Knits has been years in the making, and I am so proud and excited to be able to share my love of knitting for babies through these lovely small projects.

I'm hoping you find joy in knitting for all of your pint-sized kindred spirits.

Susan

Lark.

Plump and buoyant, **Lark** is the perfect worsted weight yarn. It's well balanced for tidy stitches and a smooth, even fabric.

It has a slight halo, a soft, squishable hand, and body enough to showcase pretty texture stitches.
Lark comes in 65 colors to color your favorite Fair Isle patterns.

And best of all, Lark is spun in the US from fine American wool.

the patterns

Basic Baby Cardigan

Finished measurements

16¾ (18¼, 19¾)" [42.5 (46.5, 50) cm] chest circumference, to fit sizes 0-3 (6-12, 12-18) months; shown in smallest size

Yarn

Lark by Quince & Co (100% American wool; 134yd [123m]/50g)

• 2 skeins Snap Pea 130

Note: Largest size uses all of two skeins. Consider purchasing an extra skein to avoid running out.

Needles

• One 24" circular needle in size US 7 [4.5 mm]
• One set double-pointed needles in size US 7 [4.5 mm]

Or size to obtain gauge

Notions

• Stitch markers
• Locking stitch markers
• Waste yarn
• Tapestry needle
• Sewing needle and matching thread
• ¾-1" [19-25 mm] buttons

Note: Number of buttons required will depend on body length and personal preference; sample shown with 6 buttons.

Gauge

22 sts and 30 rows = 4" [10 cm] in stockinette stitch, after blocking.

Note

Cardigan is worked from the top down with front neck and raglan shaping and long, fitted sleeves. Stitches are picked up along fronts and neck edge and worked in a rib trim.

Top-down raglan shaping means beginning your sweater at the neck edge, then shaping the yoke by increasing at four points: where each front of the cardigan meets a sleeve at the front shoulder, and where each sleeve meets the back at the shoulder.

Once you've worked enough increases so that body and sleeves are the proper size and yoke is deep enough, you will separate the body and sleeve stitches and work each separately.

Cardigan

With circular needle (circ) and using the long-tail cast on, CO 1 st for front, place marker (pm), CO 6 (8, 10) sts for sleeve, pm, CO 20 (22, 24) sts for back, pm, CO 6 (8, 10) sts for sleeve, pm, CO 1 st for front—34 (40, 46) sts on needle. Do not join.

> You are casting on all the stitches you need to begin the back and two sleeves, plus one stitch at each end to get the fronts started. Markers are placed at the four points of the raglan, to guide the yoke shaping.

Begin raglan set up

First row *inc set up row 1:* (RS) K1-f/b, slip marker (sl m), *k1-f/b, knit to 1 st before marker (m), k1-f/b, sl m; rep from * two more times, k1-f/b (8 sts inc'd)— 42 (48, 54) sts.
Next row: Purl.

> To shape the raglan yoke, you increase on either side of each marker, increasing one stitch in each front, two stitches in each sleeve, and two stitches in the back.

Begin front and raglan shaping

Next row *inc set up row 2:* (RS) (K1-f/b) two times, sl m, *k1-f/b, knit to 1 st before m, k1-f/b, sl m; rep from * two more times, (k1-f/b) two times (10 sts inc'd)—52 (58, 64) sts.
Next row: Purl.

The fronts of your cardigan are shaped with increases as you work your raglan shaping, creating a little scoop in the neck shaping. Front shaping can begin once you have two stitches for each front. This increase row is setting up the front shaping and continuing shaping for the raglan, so now you are increasing two stitches in each section of the yoke: fronts, sleeves, and back.

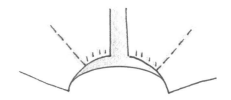

Next row *inc row:* (RS) *K1-f/b, knit to 1 st before m, k1-f/b, sl m; rep from * three more times, k1-f/b, knit to last st, k1-f/b (10 sts inc'd)—62 (68, 74) sts. Rep *inc row* every RS row 2 (5, 8) more times—82 (118, 154) sts on needle; 10 (16, 22) sts each front, 16 (24, 32) sts each sleeve, and 30 (38, 46) sts for back.
Next row: (WS) Purl.
Place a locking st marker at the beg and end of this row for button band placement.

> Front increases are continued until the fronts of your cardigan almost meet in the middle (the button band with fill in the last of the gap). The front neck scoop created gets a little bit deeper for each size.

Continue raglan shaping

Next row *inc row:* *Knit to 1 st before m, k1-f/b, sl m, k1-f/b; rep from * three more times, knit to end (8 sts inc'd)— 90 (126, 162) sts.

> The front neck shaping is complete, but you must continue the raglan yoke shaping until body and sleeves are big enough. Locking stitch markers placed at the beginning and end of this row will help with button band placement later.

Rep *inc row* every RS row 7 (5, 3) more times—146 (166, 186) sts on needle; 18 (22, 26) sts each front, 32 (36, 40) sts each sleeve, and 46 (50, 54) sts for back.

Next row: (WS) Purl.

Piece meas approx 3½ (3¾, 4)" [9, (9.5, 10) cm] from beg, measured straight down from center back.

> Once your raglan shaping is complete, you have enough stitches for body and sleeves, and the yoke is deep enough to fit comfortably.

Separate body and sleeves

Next row: (RS) *Knit to m, remove m, place sts to next m onto waste yarn for sleeve, remove m, using the backward loop cast on, CO 1 st; rep from * one more time, knit to end—84 (96, 108) sts on needle.

Next row: Purl.

Body and sleeves are now separated and sleeve stitches are placed on hold while you work the body. The markers guide you across the row: knit only the stitches for the body, and slip the sleeve stitches onto waste yarn, unworked. A single stitch is cast on at each underarm as you join front stitches to back.

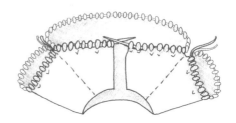

Cont in St st until pc meas 3¾ (4, 4¼)" [9.5 (10, 11) cm] from underarm, ending after a WS row.

Next row *dec row:* (RS) K1, k2tog, knit to last 3 sts, ssk, k1 (2 sts dec'd)—82 (94, 106) sts rem.

> As you reach the end of your body, before you begin the rib trim, you need to adjust your stitch count so that your ribbing can be balanced. Here, that means decreasing two stitches, one near the front edge of each side. This will leave you with a multiple of four stitches plus two, just what you need for a nicely balanced rib trim.

Rib trim

Next row: (WS) *P2, k2; rep from * to last 2 sts, p2.

Next row: *K2, p2; rep from * to last 2 sts, k2.

Cont in rib for 2 more rnds.
Next row: (WS) Bind off in pattern.

Sleeves

For instructions on making a wider sleeve, see page 25, then return here for cuff trim. K1-f/b at the beg of the final rnd for a balanced cuff trim.

Place sts held for sleeve onto double-pointed needles, pick up and knit 1 st in CO at underarm, place a locking st marker into the first st for beg of rnd—33 (37, 41) sts on needles.

> Now it's time to return to the sleeves. Held stitches are slipped onto double-pointed needles so you can work in the round. A stitch is picked up in the one cast on in the body underarm.

Begin sleeve shaping

Next rnd *dec rnd:* K1, k2tog, knit to last 2 sts, ssk (2 sts dec'd)—31 (35, 39) sts rem.

> Sleeves are shaped by decreasing on the underside of the sleeve, two stitches per decrease row.

Rep *dec rnd* every 6 (8, 10) rnds three more times—25 (29, 33) sts rem.
Work even in St st until sleeve meas 4 (5, 6)" [10 (12.5, 15) cm] from underarm.

> Decreases are worked at an even rate along the length of the sleeve, with a bit of even knitting near the end.

Next rnd *dec rnd:* *K2, p2; rep from * to last 5 sts, k2, p2tog, p1 (1 st dec'd)—24 (28, 32) sts rem.

> Before you can work your cuff trim, you need to adjust your stitch count so the rib trim lines up. Here, that means decreasing one stitch at the underside of the cuff so you have a multiple of four stitches.

Cuff trim

Next rnd: *K2, p2; rep from * to end.
Cont in rib for 2 more rnds.
Next rnd: Bind off loosely in pattern.

Finishing

Weave in ends. Steam- or wet-block cardigan to finished measurements, keeping button band markers in place.

> As you weave in your ends, use the yarn tails at underarms to close up any gaps where body and sleeves meet. The markers for button band placement must remain in place, so take care while blocking that they don't snag the fabric.

Button band

With RS facing and circ, beg at marker placed on left front, pick up and knit approx 2 sts for every 3 rows to end, making sure to pick up a multiple of 4 sts + 2.

For a great illustrated tutorial on picking up stitches along a side edge, visit our blog: www.quinceandco.com.

Pick up in this manner until you reach the end of the fabric, making sure to pick up in the last two rows. Count how many stitches you have on the needle. You will need a multiple of four stitches plus two for a balanced rib. You may need to add two stitches or add or remove one stitch to achieve a proper count.

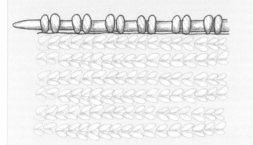

If you have an odd number of stitches, you will either need to add one stitch or remove one to achieve the correct multiple.

Does your stitch count plus one become a multiple of four? If so, you need to remove one picked up stitch: Carefully slip the last three picked up stitches off the needle. Skip one row, then pick up two stitches.

Does your stitch count minus one become a multiple of four? If so, you need to add one stitch: Slip stitches off the needle, one at a time, until you reach the gap made when you skipped a row. Pick up one stitch in each row to the end.

If you have a multiple of four stitches, you need to add two stitches: Slip stitches off the needle until you reach the first gap, then keep removing stitches until you reach the next gap. Pick up one stitch in each row to the end.

After reworking the end of your pick up, count your stitches again to make sure you have the correct multiple.

First row: (WS) *P2, k2; rep from * to last 2 sts, p2.
Next row: *K2, p2; rep from * to last 2 sts, k2.

Cont in rib for 2 more rows.
Next row: (WS) Bind off in pattern.

Buttonhole band

With RS facing and circ, beg at lower edge of right front, pick up and knit approx 2 sts for every 3 rows to marker, making sure to pick up the same number as for button band.
First row: (WS) *P2, k2; rep from * to last 2 sts, p2.
Next row: *K2, p2; rep from * to last 2 sts, k2.

Buttonhole placement

With WS facing, place a locking st marker 1 st away from neck edge, then place markers for buttonholes as you like, being sure to place after two purl sts as shown in illustration. Note that first marker is between two purl stitches.
Place your markers as you like: from neck edge all the way to hem, or only three buttons in the yoke; close together, or spread apart. Use your finished button band to try out your placement. Make sure your buttons will not overlap.

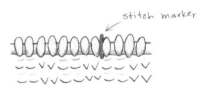

stitch marker

Next row *buttonhole row:* (WS) P1, remove m, yo, k2tog, k1, *work in rib to m, remove m, yo, k2tog; rep from * for each marker, work in rib to end.

Next row: *K2, p2; rep from * to last 2 sts, k2.
Next row: Bind off in pattern.

Neck trim

With RS facing and circ, beg at right front neck edge, pick up and knit 50 (62, 74) sts along neck edge as follows: 3 sts in side edge of each button band, 4 (7, 10) sts along each front neck edge, 1 st in each CO st and 1 st in each raglan line along shoulders and back neck.

For a great illustrated tutorial on picking up stitches in a cast on edge, visit our blog: www.quinceandco.com.

First row: (WS) *P2, k2; rep from * to last 2 sts, p2.
Next row: *K2, p2; rep from * to last 2 sts, k2.
Cont in rib for 1 more row.
Next row: (RS) Bind off in pattern.

Sew buttons opposite buttonholes. Weave in remaining ends and block again, if you like.

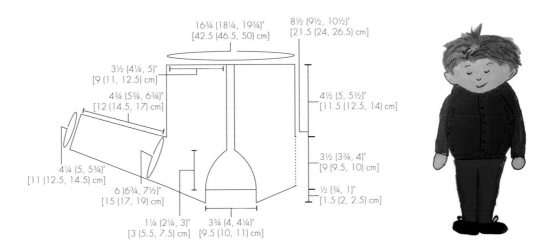

16¾ (18¼, 19¾)"
[42.5 (46.5, 50) cm]

8½ (9½, 10½)"
[21.5 (24, 26.5) cm]

3½ (4¼, 5)"
[9 (11, 12.5) cm]

4¾ (5¾, 6¾)"
[12 (14.5, 17) cm]

4½ (5, 5½)"
[11.5 (12.5, 14) cm]

4¼ (5, 5¾)"
[11 (12.5, 14.5) cm]

3½ (3¾, 4)"
[9 (9.5, 10) cm]

6 (6¾, 7½)"
[15 (17, 19) cm]

½ (¾, 1)"
[1.5 (2, 2.5) cm]

1¼ (2¼, 3)"
[3 (5.5, 7.5) cm]

3¾ (4, 4¼)"
[9.5 (10, 11) cm]

Striped Short-sleeved Cardigan

Finished measurements

16¾ (18¼, 19¾)" [42.5 (46.5, 50) cm] chest circumference, to fit sizes 0-3 (6-12, 12-18) months; shown in smallest size

Yarn

Lark by Quince & Co (100% American wool; 134yd [123m]/50g)
- 1 skein Snap Pea 130 (A)
- 1 skein Leek 131 (B)
- 1 skein Parsley 129 (C)

Needles
- One 24" circular needle in size US 7 [4.5 mm]
- One set double-pointed needles in size US 7 [4.5 mm]

Or size to obtain gauge

Notions
- Stitch markers
- Locking stitch markers
- Waste yarn
- Tapestry needle
- Sewing needle and matching thread
- ¾-1" [19-25 mm] buttons

Note: Number of buttons required will depend on body length and personal preference; sample shown with 6 buttons.

Gauge

22 sts and 30 rows = 4" [10 cm] in stockinette stitch, after blocking.

Stripe pattern

Row 1: (RS) With A, knit.
Row 2: With A, purl.
Row 3: With B, knit.
Row 4: With B, purl.
Row 5: With C, knit.
Row 6: With C, purl.
Repeat Rows 1-6 for stripe pattern.

Note

Cardigan is worked from the top down with front neck and raglan shaping and short sleeves. Stitches are picked up along fronts and neck edge and worked in a rib trim.

Cardigan

With A and circular needle (circ), using the long-tail cast on, CO 1 st for front, place marker (pm), CO 6 (8, 10) sts for sleeve, pm, CO 20 (22, 24) sts for back, pm, CO 6 (8, 10) sts for sleeve, pm, CO 1 st for front—34 (40, 46) sts on needle. Do not join.

Begin raglan set up and stripe pattern

First row *inc row:* (RS) K1-f/b, slip marker (sl m), *k1-f/b, knit to 1 st before marker (m), k1-f/b, sl m; rep from * two more times, k1-f/b (8 sts inc'd)—42 (48, 54) sts. This is Row 1 of stripe pattern; cont in stripe pattern throughout yoke.

Next row: Purl.

Begin front and raglan shaping

Next row *inc set up row 2:* (RS) (K1-f/b) two times, sl m, *k1-f/b, knit to 1 st before m, k1-f/b, sl m; rep from * two more times, (k1-f/b) two times (10 sts inc'd)—52 (58, 64) sts.

Next row: Purl.

Next row *inc row:* (RS) *K1-f/b, knit to 1 st before m, k1-f/b, sl m; rep from * three more times, k1-f/b, knit to last st, k1-f/b (10 sts inc'd)—62 (68, 74) sts. Cont in stripe patt and rep *inc row* every RS row 2 (5, 8) more times—82 (118, 154) sts on needle; 10 (16, 22) sts each front, 16 (24, 32) sts each sleeve, and 30 (38, 46) sts for back.

Next row: (WS) Purl.

Place a locking st marker at the beg and end of this row for button band placement.

Continue raglan shaping

Next row *inc row:* *Knit to 1 st before m, k1-f/b, sl m, k1-f/b; rep from * three more times, knit to end (8 sts inc'd)—90 (126, 162) sts.

Rep *inc row* every RS row 7 (5, 3) more times—146 (166, 186) sts on needle; 18 (22, 26) sts each front, 32 (36, 40) sts each sleeve, and 46 (50, 54) sts for back.

Next row: (WS) Purl.

Piece meas approx 3½ (3¾, 4)" [9 (9.5, 10) cm] from beg, measured straight down from center back.

Separate body and sleeves

Continue in stripe pattern.

Next row: (RS) *Knit to m, remove m, place sts to next m onto waste yarn for sleeve, remove m, using the backward loop cast on, CO 1 st; rep from * one more time, knit to end—84 (96, 108) sts on needle.

Next row: Purl.

Cont in stripe patt until pc meas 3¾ (4, 4¼)" [9.5 (10, 11) cm] from underarm, ending after Row 3 of stripe.

Next row *dec row:* (RS) With B, k1, k2tog, knit to last 3 sts, ssk, k1 (2 sts dec'd)—82 (94, 106) sts rem. Break A and B; cont with C.

Rib trim

Next row: (WS) *P2, k2; rep from * to last 2 sts, p2.

Next row: *K2, p2; rep from * to last 2 sts, k2.

Cont in rib for 2 more rows.
Next row: (WS) Bind off in pattern.

Sleeves

To make long sleeves, cont in stripe pattern, knitting every round. See page 13 for fitted, or page 25 for wide sleeves, then change to C and return here for cuff trim. For wide sleeves, k1-f/b at the beg of final rnd for a balanced cuff trim. For fitted sleeves, work dec rnd below.

Place sts held for sleeve onto double-pointed needles. With RS facing and C, pick up and knit 1 st in CO at underarm, place a locking st marker into the first st for beg of rnd—33 (37, 41) sts on needles. Cont with C.

Next rnd *dec rnd:* *K2, p2; rep from * to last 5 sts, k2, p2tog, p1 (1 st dec'd)—32 (36, 40) sts rem.

Cuff trim

Next rnd: *K2, p2; rep from * to end.
Cont in rib for 2 more rnds.
Next rnd: Bind off loosely in pattern.

Finishing

Weave in ends. Steam- or wet-block cardigan to finished measurements, keeping button band markers in place.

Button band

With RS facing, circ, and C, beg at marker placed on left front, pick up and knit approx 2 sts for every 3 rows to end, making sure to pick up a multiple of 4 sts + 2.

First row: (WS) *P2, k2; rep from * to last 2 sts, p2.
Next row: *K2, p2; rep from * to last 2 sts, k2.
Cont in rib for 2 more rows.
Next row: (WS) Bind off in pattern.

Buttonhole band

With RS facing, circ, and C, beg at lower edge of right front, pick up and knit approx 2 sts for every 3 rows to marker, making sure to pick up the same number as for button band.
First row: (WS) *P2, k2; rep from * to last 2 sts, p2.
Next row: *K2, p2; rep from * to last 2 sts, k2.

Buttonhole placement

With WS facing, place a locking st marker 1 st away from neck edge, then place markers for buttonholes as you like, being sure to place after two purl sts as shown in illustration, page 14. Note that first marker is between two purl stitches.

Next row *buttonhole row:* (WS) P1, remove m, yo, k2tog, k1, *work in rib to m, remove m, yo, k2tog; rep from * for each marker, work in rib to end.
Next row: *K2, p2; rep from * to last 2 sts, k2.
Next row: (WS) Bind off in pattern.

Neck trim

With RS facing, circ, and C, beg at right front neck edge, pick up and knit 50 (62, 74) sts along neck edge as follows: 3 sts in side edge of each button band, 4 (7, 10) sts along each front neck edge, 1 st in each CO st and 1 st in each raglan line along shoulders and back neck.

First row: (WS) *P2, k2; rep from * to last 2 sts, p2.

Next row: *K2, p2; rep from * to last 2 sts, k2.

Cont in rib for 1 more row.

Next row: (RS) Bind off in pattern.

Sew buttons opposite buttonholes. Weave in remaining ends and block again, if you like.

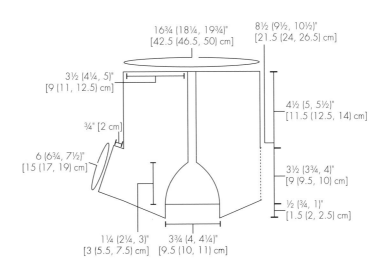

16¾ (18¼, 19¾)"
[42.5 (46.5, 50) cm]

8½ (9½, 10½)"
[21.5 (24, 26.5) cm]

3½ (4¼, 5)"
[9 (11, 12.5) cm]

4½ (5, 5½)"
[11.5 (12.5, 14) cm]

¾" [2 cm]

6 (6¾, 7½)"
[15 (17, 19) cm]

3½ (3¾, 4)"
[9 (9.5, 10) cm]

½ (¾, 1)"
[1.5 (2, 2.5) cm]

1¼ (2¼, 3)"
[3 (5.5, 7.5) cm]

3¾ (4, 4¼)"
[9.5 (10, 11) cm]

Empire-waist Cardigan

Finished measurements
23¼ (26½, 29¾)" [59 (67.5, 75.5) cm] chest circumference, to fit sizes 0-3 (6-12, 12-18) months; shown in largest size

Yarn
Lark by Quince & Co (100% American wool; 134yd [123m]/50g)
- 2 skeins Dogwood 135

Note: Largest size will require an extra skein if choosing to work long sleeves.

Needles
- One 24" circular needle in size US 7 [4.5 mm]
- One set double-pointed needles in size US 7 [4.5 mm]

Or size to obtain gauge

Notions
- Stitch markers
- Locking stitch markers
- Waste yarn
- Tapestry needle
- Sewing needle and matching thread
- ¾-1" [19-25 mm] buttons

Note: Number of buttons required will depend on body length and personal preference; sample shown with 2 buttons.

Gauge
22 sts and 30 rows = 4" [10 cm] in stockinette stitch, after blocking.

Note
Cardigan is worked from the top down with front neck and raglan shaping, short sleeves, and an empire waist. Stitches are picked up along fronts and neck edge and worked in a seed stitch trim.

Cardigan
With circular needle (circ) and using the long-tail cast on, CO 1 st for front, place marker (pm), CO 6 (8, 10) sts for sleeve, pm, CO 20 (22, 24) sts for back, pm, CO 6 (8, 10) sts for sleeve, pm, CO 1 st for front—34 (40, 46) sts on needle. Do not join.

Begin raglan set up
First row *inc set up row 1:* (RS) K1-f/b, slip marker (sl m), *k1-f/b, knit to 1 st before marker (m), k1-f/b, sl m; rep from * two more times, k1-f/b (8 sts inc'd)—42 (48, 54) sts.
Next row: Purl.

Begin front and raglan shaping
Next row *inc set up row 2:* (RS) (K1-f/b) two times, sl m, *k1-f/b, knit to 1 st before m, k1-f/b, sl m; rep from * two more times, (k1-f/b) two times (10 sts inc'd)—52 (58, 64) sts.

Next row: Purl.

Next row *inc row:* *K1-f/b, knit to 1 st before m, k1-f/b, sl m; rep from * three more times, k1-f/b, knit to last st, k1-f/b (10 sts inc'd)—62 (68, 74) sts.

Rep *inc row* every RS row 2 (5, 8) more times—82 (118, 154) sts on needle; 10 (16, 22) sts each front, 16 (24, 32) sts each sleeve, and 30 (38, 46) sts for back.

Next row: (WS) Purl.

Place a locking st marker at the beg and end of this row for button band placement.

Continue raglan shaping

Next row *inc row:* (RS) *Knit to 1 st before m, k1-f/b, sl m, k1-f/b; rep from * three more times, knit to end (8 sts inc'd)—90 (126, 162) sts.

Rep *inc row* every RS row 7 (5, 3) more times— 146 (166, 186) sts on needle; 18 (22, 26) sts each front, 32 (36, 40) sts each sleeve, and 46 (50, 54) sts for back.

Next row: (WS) Purl.

Piece meas approx 3½ (3¾, 4)" [9, (9.5, 10) cm] from beg, measured straight down from center back.

Separate body and sleeves

Next row: (RS) *Knit to m, remove m, place sts to next m onto waste yarn for sleeve, remove m, using the backward loop cast on, CO 1 st; rep from * one more time, knit to end—84 (96, 108) sts on needle.

Next row: Knit.

Begin empire waist

Next row *inc row:* (RS) K2, *k3, (k1, yo, k1) into next st; rep from * to last 2 sts, k1-f/b, k1; 41 (47, 53) sts inc'd— 125 (143, 161) sts.

Next row: Purl.

Cont in St st until pc meas 3¾ (4, 4¼)" [9.5 (10, 11) cm] from underarm, ending after a WS row.

Seed stitch trim

Next row: (RS) *K1, p1; rep from * to last st, k1.

Cont in seed st for 3 more rows.

Next rnd: (RS) Bind off loosely in pattern.

Sleeves

To make long sleeves, see page 13 for fitted, or page 25 for wide sleeves, then return here for cuff trim. Do not increase or decrease before trim; end with an odd number of stitches.

Place sts held for sleeve onto double-pointed needles, pick up and knit 1 st in CO at underarm, place a locking st marker into the first st for beg of rnd—33 (37, 41) sts on needles.

Cuff trim

Next rnd: *K1, p1; rep from * to last st, k1.

Next rnd: *P1, k1; rep from * to last st, p1.

Cont in seed st for 2 more rows.

Next rnd: Bind off loosely in pattern.

Finishing

Weave in ends. Steam- or wet-block cardigan to finished measurements, keeping button band markers in place.

Button band

With RS facing and circ, beg at marker placed on left front, pick up and knit approx 2 sts for every 3 rows to end, making sure to pick up an even number of stitches.

First row: (WS) *K1, p1; rep from * to end.
Next row: *P1, k1; rep from * to end.
Work 1 more row in seed st.
Next row: (RS) Bind off in pattern.

Buttonhole band

With RS facing and circ, beg at lower edge of right front, pick up and knit approx 2 sts for every 3 rows to marker, making sure to pick up the same number as for button band.

Buttonhole placement

With WS facing, place a locking st marker 1 st away from neck edge, then place markers for buttonholes as you like, making sure there is an even number of stitches between each marker.

First row *buttonhole row:* (WS) K1, yo, k2tog, *(p1, k1) to m, remove m, yo, k2tog; rep from * for each marker, (p1, k1) to last st, p1.
Next row: *P1, k1; rep from * to end.
Cont in seed st for 1 more row.
Next row: (RS) Bind off in pattern.

Neck trim

With RS facing and circ, beg at right front neck edge, pick up and knit 50 (62, 74) sts along neck edge as follows: 3 sts in side edge of each button band, 4 (7, 10) sts along each front neck edge, 1 st in each CO st and 1 st in each raglan line along shoulders and back neck.

First row: (WS) *K1, p1; rep from * to end.
Next row: *P1, k1; rep from * to end.
Cont in seed st for 1 more row.
Next row: (RS) Bind off in pattern.

Sew buttons opposite buttonholes. Weave in remaining ends and block again, if you like.

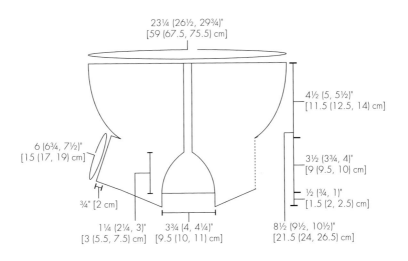

23¼ (26½, 29¾)"
[59 (67.5, 75.5) cm]

6 (6¾, 7½)"
[15 (17, 19) cm]

4½ (5, 5½)"
[11.5 (12.5, 14) cm]

3½ (3¾, 4)"
[9 (9.5, 10) cm]

½ (¾, 1)"
[1.5 (2, 2.5) cm]

¾" [2 cm]

1¼ (2¼, 3)"
[3 (5.5, 7.5) cm]

3¾ (4, 4¼)"
[9.5 (10, 11) cm]

8½ (9½, 10½)"
[21.5 (24, 26.5) cm]

Hooded Cardigan

Finished measurements

16¾ (18¼, 19¾)" [42.5 (46.5, 50) cm] chest circumference, to fit sizes 0-3 (6-12, 12-18) months; shown in middle size

Yarn

Lark by Quince & Co (100% American wool; 134yd [123m]/50g)

- 2 (2, 3) skeins Iceland 150 (A)
- 1 skein Nasturtium 136 (B)
- 1 skein Egret 101 (C)

Note: Middle size uses all of two skeins of color A. Consider purchasing an extra skein to avoid running out. Approx 20 yds of C are used. If you have Lark left-overs, use them!

Needles

- One 24" circular needle in size US 7 [4.5 mm]
- One spare circ in size US 7 [4.5 mm]
- One set double-pointed needles in size US 7 [4.5 mm]

Or size to obtain gauge

Notions

- Stitch markers
- Locking stitch markers
- Waste yarn
- Crochet hook in size US G [4 mm] (optional)
- Tapestry needle
- Sewing needle and matching thread
- 2 buttons, 1" [25 mm]

Gauge

22 sts and 30 rows = 4" [10 cm] in stockinette stitch, after blocking.

Note

Cardigan is worked from the top down with front neck and raglan shaping and long, wide sleeves. Stitches are picked up along neck edge and worked flat for a hood, then joined at top using the three-needle bind off or grafted using the Kitchener stitch. Then stitches are picked up along entire front edge and worked in a garter trim with i-cord or crochet chain button loops.

Cardigan

With A and circular needle (circ), using the long-tail cast on, CO 1 st for front, place marker (pm), CO 6 (8, 10) sts for sleeve, pm, CO 20 (22, 24) sts for back, pm, CO 6 (8, 10) sts for sleeve, pm, CO 1 st for front—34 (40, 46) sts on needle. Do not join.

Begin raglan set up

First row *inc set up row 1:* (RS) K1-f/b, slip marker (sl m), *k1-f/b, knit to 1 st before marker (m), k1-f/b, sl m; rep from * two more times, k1-f/b (8 sts inc'd)— 42 (48, 54) sts.
Next row: Purl.

Begin front and raglan shaping

Next row *inc set up row 2:* (RS) (K1-f/b) two times, sl m, *k1-f/b, knit to 1 st before m, k1-f/b, sl m; rep from * two more times, (k1-f/b) two times (10 sts inc'd)—52 (58, 64) sts.
Next row: Purl.
Next row *inc row:* *K1-f/b, knit to 1 st before m, k1-f/b, sl m; rep from * three more times, k1-f/b, knit to last st, k1-f/b (10 sts inc'd)—62 (68, 74) sts.
Rep *inc row* every RS row 2 (5, 8) more times—82 (118, 154) sts on needle; 10 (16, 22) sts each front, 16 (24, 32) sts each sleeve, and 30 (38, 46) sts for back.
Next row: (WS) Purl.
Measure 1" [2.5 cm] up from needle along neck edge and place a locking st marker at the edge of that row for hood pick-up. Repeat for other neck edge.

Continue raglan shaping

Next row *inc row:* (RS) *Knit to 1 st before m, k1-f/b, sl m, k1-f/b; rep from * three more times, knit to end (8 sts inc'd)—90 (126, 162) sts.
Rep *inc row* every RS row 7 (5, 3) more times— 146 (166, 186) sts on needle;

18 (22, 26) sts each front, 32 (36, 40) sts each sleeve, and 46 (50, 54) sts for back.
Next row: (WS) Purl.
Piece meas approx 3½ (3¾, 4)" [9, (9.5, 10) cm] from beg, measured straight down from center back.

Separate body and sleeves

Next row: (RS) *Knit to m, remove m, place sts to next m onto waste yarn for sleeve, remove m, using the backward loop cast on, CO 1 st; rep from * one more time, knit to end—84 (96, 108) sts on needle.
Next row: Purl.
Cont in St st until pc meas 3¾ (4, 4¼)" [9.5 (10, 11) cm] from underarm, ending after a WS row.
Break A and change to B.

Garter trim

Next row: (RS) Knit.
Cont in garter st for 5 more rows.
Break B and change to C.
Next row: (RS) Bind off knitwise.

Sleeves

For instructions on making a more fitted sleeve, see page 13, then return here for cuff trim.
Place sts held for sleeve onto double-pointed needles (dpns). With RS facing and A, pick up and knit 1 st in CO at underarm, place a locking st marker into the first st for beg of rnd—33 (37, 41) sts on needles.

Begin sleeve shaping

First rnd *dec rnd:* K1, k2tog, knit to last 2 sts, ssk (2 sts dec'd)—31 (35, 39) sts rem.
Rep *dec rnd* every 8 (12, 16) rnds two more times—27 (31, 35) sts rem.
Work even in St st until sleeve meas 4 (5, 6)" [10 (12.5, 15) cm] from underarm. Break A and change to B.

Cuff trim

Next rnd: Knit.
Next rnd: Purl.
Cont in garter st for 2 more rnds.
Break B and change to C.
Next rnd: Bind off loosely knitwise.

Finishing

Weave in ends. Steam- or wet-block cardigan to finished measurements, keeping hood pick-up markers in place.

Hood

With RS facing, circ, and A, beg at marker on right front neck edge, pick up and knit 42 (50, 58) sts along neck edge as follows: 3 (4, 5) sts along each front neck edge, 1 st in each CO st and 1 st in each raglan line along shoulders and back neck.
First row: (WS) Purl.
Next row: K2, k1-f/b, *k3 (4, 5), k1-f/b; rep from * to last 3 (2, 1) sts, knit to end (10 sts inc'd)—52 (60, 68) sts.

Cont in St st until hood meas 7 (7½, 8)" [18 (19, 20.5) cm] from pick-up. Do not break yarn.

To close hood by grafting:

Place 26 (30, 34) sts onto spare circ and fold hood in half with WS of pcs together. Break yarn leaving a 20" [50 cm] tail and thread onto tapestry needle. Using the Kitchener stitch, graft sides of hood together.

To close hood using the three-needle bind off:

Place 26 (30, 34) sts onto spare circ and fold hood in half with RS of pcs together. With attached yarn and using the three-needle bind off, BO all sts.

Front garter trim

With RS facing, circ, and B, beg at lower edge of right front, pick up and knit 2 sts for every 3 rows along right front, around edge of hood, and along left front to end.
First row: (WS) Knit.
Cont in garter st for 4 more rows.
Break B and change to C.
Next row: (RS) Bind off knitwise.

To make button loops with i-cord:

On right front, measure 2" [5 cm] down front edge from pick-up for hood.

With RS facing, a dpn, and C, pick up and knit 2 sts. Do not turn to WS. Slide sts to RH needle tip.

First row: K2, then slide sts to RH needle tip.

Cont working in i-cord for 2" [5 cm].

Next row: K2tog—1 st rem.

Draw yarn through rem st and sew to bound off edge beside pick-up, forming a loop.

Measure 1" [2.5 cm] down from first loop and repeat for second loop.

To make button loops with a crochet chain:

On right front, measure 2" [5 cm] down front edge from pick-up for hood.

With RS facing and C, insert hook into the bound off edge and draw up a loop.

Work ch st for 2" [5 cm].

Insert hook into bound off edge beside beg of ch and sl st, forming a loop. Fasten off.

Measure 1" [2.5 cm] down from first loop and repeat for second loop.

Sew buttons opposite buttonholes. Weave in remaining ends and block again, if you like.

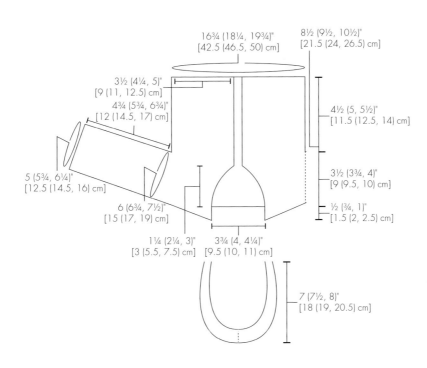

16¾ (18¼, 19¾)"
[42.5 (46.5, 50) cm]

8½ (9½, 10½)"
[21.5 (24, 26.5) cm]

3½ (4¼, 5)"
[9 (11, 12.5) cm]

4¾ (5¾, 6¾)"
[12 (14.5, 17) cm]

4½ (5, 5½)"
[11.5 (12.5, 14) cm]

5 (5¾, 6¼)"
[12.5 (14.5, 16) cm]

3½ (3¾, 4)"
[9 (9.5, 10) cm]

½ (¾, 1)"
[1.5 (2, 2.5) cm]

6 (6¾, 7½)"
[15 (17, 19) cm]

1¼ (2¼, 3)"
[3 (5.5, 7.5) cm]

3¾ (4, 4¼)"
[9.5 (10, 11) cm]

7 (7½, 8)"
[18 (19, 20.5) cm]

Leaf-top Baby Hat

Finished measurements
11 (13, 14½)" [28 (33, 37) cm] brim circumference and 5¼ (6¼, 6¾)" [13.5 (16, 17) cm] tall, to fit sizes 0-3 (6-12, 12-18) months; shown in middle size

Yarn
Lark by Quince & Co (100% American wool; 134yd [123m]/50g)
- 1 skein Snap Pea 128 (A)
- 1 skein Bark 121 (B)
- 1 skein Parsley 129 (C)

Note: Approx 5 yds each of B and C are used. If you have Lark leftovers, use them!

Needles
- One set double-pointed needles in size US 7 [4.5 mm]

Or size to obtain gauge

Notions
- Locking stitch marker
- Stitch markers
- Waste yarn
- Tapestry needle

Gauge
22 sts and 32 rnds = 4" [10 cm] in stockinette stitch, after blocking.

Note
Hat is knitted from the bottom up, in the round. Leaf tops are worked from remaining crown stitches on separate i-cord stems, then wrapped together.

Hat
With A and using the long-tail cast on, CO 60 (72, 80) sts. Join to work in the rnd, careful not to twist sts. Place a removable st marker into the first st for beg of rnd.

Begin ribbed trim
First rnd: *K2, p2; rep from * to end. Cont in rib for 5 more rnds.

Sizes 11 (-, 14½)" [28 (-, 37) cm] only:
Proceed to All sizes.

Size - (13, -)" [- (33, -) cm] only:
Next rnd *dec rnd:* K2tog, knit to last 2 sts, k2tog (2 sts dec'd)—70 sts rem.

All sizes
Next rnd: Knit.

Cont in St st until hat meas 4 (5, 5½)" [10 (13, 14) cm] from beg.

Next rnd *place marker:* *K10, place marker; rep from * to end.

Begin crown shaping
Next rnd *dec rnd 1:* *Knit to 2 sts before m, k2tog; rep from * to end; 6 (7, 8) sts dec'd—54 (63, 72) sts rem.

Rep *dec rnd 1* every 2 rnds three more times, every 3 rnds one time, then every rnd one time—24 (28, 32) sts rem.

Next rnd *dec rnd 2:* *K2tog; rep from * to end—12 (14, 16) sts rem.

Next rnd: Knit.

Next rnd: Rep *dec rnd 2*—6 (7, 8) sts rem. Break A.

If you wish to have a hat with a simple crown, using a tapestry needle, draw yarn through remaining stitches and cinch closed. If working a leaf top, change to B.

First leaf top
Next rnd: With B, k2, then place rem sts onto waste yarn. Do not turn to WS. Slide sts to RH needle tip.

First row: K2, then slide sts to RH needle tip. Cont in i-cord for 1" [2.5 cm]. Break B and change to C.

Begin leaf
Begin working back and forth on two dpns.

Row 1 *inc row:* (RS) K1, m1, k1 (1 st inc'd)—3 sts.

Row 2 and all WS rows: Purl.

Row 3 *inc row:* K1, yo, k1, yo, k1 (2 sts inc'd)—5 sts.

Row 5 *inc row:* K2, yo, k1, yo, k2 (2 sts inc'd)—7 sts.

Row 7 *dec row:* K1, ssk, k1, k2tog, k1 (2 sts dec'd)—5 sts.

Row 9 *dec row:* Ssk, k1, k2tog (2 sts dec'd)—3 sts.

Row 11 *dec row:* K3tog (2 sts dec'd)—1 st rem.

Break yarn and draw through rem st.

Second leaf top
Return next 2 (2, 3) sts to a dpn and join B, ready to work a RS row.

Sizes 11 (13, -)" [28 (33, -) cm] only:
Work i-cord and leaf for second leaf same as for first.

Size - (-, 14½)" [- (-, 37) cm] only:
Next row *dec row:* (RS) K2tog, k1—2 sts rem. Work i-cord and leaf for second leaf same as for first.

Third leaf top
Return next 2 (3, 3) sts to a dpn and join B, ready to work a RS row.

Size 11 (-, -)" [28 (-, -) cm] only:
Work i-cord and leaf for third leaf same as for first.

Sizes - (13, 14½)" [- (33, 37) cm] only:
Next row *dec row:* K2tog, k1—2 sts rem.
Work i-cord and leaf for third leaf same
as for first.

Begin leaf base
Cut an approx 24" [60 cm] length of B
and thread onto tapestry needle. Keeping a 6" [15 cm] tail, hold yarn against
crown of hat and wrap around all three
i-cord stems until stems are wrapped
for half of their length and base is thick
enough to stand up. Draw tapestry
needle down through the wrapped base
to WS of hat.

Finishing
Weave in ends. Steam- or wet-block hat
to finished measurements.

Sweet Leaf Blanket

Finished measurements
32¼" [82 cm] wide and 30¾" [78 cm] long

Yarn
Lark by Quince & Co (100% American wool; 134yd [123m]/50g)
- 7 skeins Snap Pea 130

Needles
- One 32" circular needle in size US 8 [5 mm]

Or size to obtain gauge

Notions
- Stitch markers
- Tapestry needle

Gauge
20 sts and 29 rows = 4" [10 cm] in stockinette stitch, after blocking.

Leaf panel (25 stitches)
Row 1: (RS) K1, M1L, skp, k4, k2tog, k3, M1R, k1, M1L, k3, skp, k4, k2tog, M1R, k1.

Row 2 and all WS rows: Purl.

Row 3: K1, M1L, k1, skp, k2, k2tog, k4, M1R, k1, M1L, k4, skp, k2, k2tog, k1, M1R, k1.

Row 5: K1, M1L, k2, skp, k2tog, k5, M1R, k1, M1L, k5, skp, k2tog, k2, M1L, k1.

Row 7: K1, M1L, k3, skp, k4, k2tog, M1R, k1, M1L, skp, k4, k2tog, k3, M1R, k1.

Row 9: K1, M1L, k4, skp, k2, k2tog, k1, M1R, k1, M1L, k1, skp, k2, k2tog, k4, M1R, k1.

Row 11: K1, M1L, k5, skp, k2tog, k2, M1R, k1, M1L, k2, skp, k2tog, k5, M1R, k1.

Row 12: (WS) Purl.

Repeat Rows 1-12 for leaf panel.

Note
Blanket is worked flat lengthwise. Garter trim is worked at the same time.

Blanket
Using the long-tail cast on, CO 161 sts. Do not join.

Begin garter trim
First row: (RS) Knit.

Cont in garter st for 2 more rows.

Next row *place markers:* (WS) K3, p25, place marker for panel (pm), p40, pm, p25, pm, p40, pm, p25, k3 sts to end.

Begin stockinette and leaf panels
Next row: (RS) K3, *work Row 1 of leaf panel to marker (m), slip marker (sl m), knit to next m; rep from * one more time, work Row 1 of leaf panel to last 3 sts, k3.
Next row: K3, purl to last 3 sts, k3.
Cont as est, in St st with leaf panels and garter st edges, until Rows 1-12 have been worked a total of 18 times.

Begin garter trim
Next row: (RS) Knit.
Cont in garter st for 3 more rows.
Next row: (RS) Bind off loosely knitwise.

Finishing
Weave in ends. Steam- or wet-block blanket to finished measurements.

Key

□ knit on RS, purl on WS

⅂ M1L

ℾ M1R

◺ skp

◹ k2tog

Leaf panel

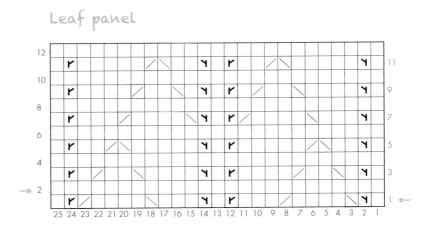

Doll Cardigan

Finished measurements
14" [35.5 cm] chest circumference, to fit an 18" doll or small teddy bear

Yarn
Lark by Quince & Co (100% American wool; 134yd [123m]/50g)

- 1 skein; shown in Sorbet 117 and Apricot 137

Needles
- One 24" circular needle in size US 7 [4.5 mm]
- One set double-pointed needles in size US 7 [4.5 mm]

Or size to obtain gauge

Notions
- Stitch markers
- Locking stitch marker
- Waste yarn
- Tapestry needle
- Sewing needle and matching thread
- 3 buttons, approx ½" [13 mm]

Gauge
22 sts and 30 rows = 4" [10 cm] in stockinette stitch, after blocking.

Special abbreviation
sl 1: Slip next stitch purlwise with yarn to the WS of work.

Note
Cardigan is worked from the top down with raglan shaping. Sleeves are worked in the round to cuff.

Cardigan
With circular needle and using the long-tail cast on, CO 44 sts. Do not join.

Begin neck trim
First row: (RS) Knit.
Cont in garter st for 2 more rows.
Next row *place markers:* (WS) K10, place marker (pm), k2, pm, k20, pm, k2, pm, k10 sts to end.

Begin raglan shaping
Row 1 *inc row:* (RS) Sl 1, *knit to marker (m), k1-f/b, slip marker (sl m), k1-f/b; rep from * three more times, knit to end (8 sts inc'd)—52 sts.
Row 2 and all WS rows: Sl 1, k2, purl to last 3 sts, k3.
Row 3 *buttonhole row:* Work *inc row* to last 3 sts, yo, k2tog, k1 (8 sts inc'd)—60 sts.

Row 5: Rep *inc row*—68 sts.
Row 6: (WS) Rep Row 2.
Rep Rows 1-6 one more time, then work Rows 1-4 one time—108 sts on needle; 18 sts for each front and each sleeve and 36 sts for back.

Separate body and sleeves

Next row: (RS) Sl 1, knit to m, remove m, place sts for sleeve onto waste yarn, remove m, using the backward loop cast on, CO 2 sts, knit across back sts, remove m, place 18 sleeve sts onto waste yarn, remove m, CO 2 sts, knit to end—76 sts on needle.

Body

Next row: (WS) Sl 1, k2, purl to last 3 sts, k3.
Next row: Sl 1, knit to end.
Cont as est until body meas 2" [5 cm] from underarm, ending after a WS row.

Begin garter trim

Next row: (RS) Knit.
Cont in garter st for 3 more rows.
Next row: (RS) Loosely bind off knitwise.

Sleeves

Place sts held for sleeves onto dpns. Pick up and knit 1 st in first st CO at underarm, pm for beg of rnd, pick up and knit 1 st in rem CO st, knit to end—20 sts. Place a locking st marker into first st for beg of rnd.
Next rnd: Knit.
Cont in St st until sleeve meas 2" [5 cm] from underarm.

Cuff trim

Next rnd: Purl.
Cont in garter st for 2 more rnds.
Next rnd: Bind off loosely knitwise.

Finishing

Weave in ends. Steam- or wet-block cardigan to finished measurements.
Sew buttons opposite buttonholes.

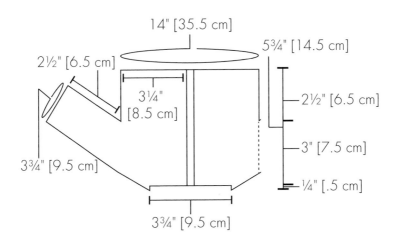

14" [35.5 cm]

5¾" [14.5 cm]

2½" [6.5 cm]

3¼" [8.5 cm]

2½" [6.5 cm]

3" [7.5 cm]

¼" [.5 cm]

3¾" [9.5 cm]

3¾" [9.5 cm]

Finished measurements

3" [7.5 cm] tall and 6" [15 cm] wide

Yarn

Lark by Quince & Co (100% American wool; 134yd [123m]/50g)

- Pullover 1 in Winesap 133 and Egret 101
- Pullover 2 in Nasturtium 136
- Cardigan 1 in Kumlien's Gull 152
- Cardigan 2 in Carrie's Yellow 125 and Kumlien's Gull 152

Note: Approx 25 yds used for each sweater. If you have leftovers of Lark, use them!

Needles

- One set double-pointed needles in size US 7 [4.5 mm]

Or size to obtain gauge

Notions

- Locking stitch marker
- Stitch markers
- Waste yarn
- Tapestry needle

optional

- Sewing needle and matching thread
- Approx ¼" [6 mm] buttons

Gauge

22 sts and 30 rows = 4" [10 cm] in stockinette stitch, after blocking. *Achieving exact gauge isn't essential for this project.*

Notes

Ornaments are knitted seamlessly from the top down. Pullover is worked in the round. Cardigan yoke and body are worked flat on two double-pointed needles, or use a 24" circular needle, if you prefer.

Pullover

Using the long-tail cast on, CO 12 sts. Arrange sts onto 4 double-pointed needles (dpns) as follows:

Needle 1 (N1): 4 sts for front;
Needle 2 (N2): 2 sts for sleeve;
Needle 3 (N3): 4 sts for back;
Needle 4 (N4): 2 sts for sleeve.

Join to work in the rnd, careful not to twist sts. Place a locking st marker into the first st for beg of rnd.

Begin at neck edge

First rnd: Knit.
Next rnd: Purl.

Begin raglan shaping

Next rnd *inc rnd:* *K1-f/b, knit to last st on needle, k1-f/b; rep from * for each needle (8 sts inc'd)—20 sts.
Next rnd: Knit.

Rep *inc rnd* every other rnd three more times—44 sts on needles; 12 sts each for front and back and 10 sts for each sleeve.

Separate body and sleeves
Next rnd: Knit across N1, place sts from N2 onto waste yarn, using the backward loop cast on, CO 1 st to N1, knit across N3, place sts from N4 onto waste yarn, CO 1 st to N3—26 sts on needles. Arrange sts onto 3 dpns as follows: **N1:** 10 sts; **N2:** 10 sts; **N3:** 6 sts. Place a removable st marker into the first st for BOR.
Next rnd: Knit.
Cont in St st until body meas 1½" [4 cm] from underarm.

For garter stitch trim *(shown in pullover 1):*
Next rnd: Purl.
Cont in garter st for 2 more rnds.
Next rnd: Bind off loosely knitwise.

For ribbed trim *(shown in pullover 2):*
Next rnd: *K1, p1; rep from * to end.
Cont in rib for 1 more rnd.
Next rnd: Bind off loosely knitwise.

Sleeves
Arrange sts for sleeve onto 3 dpns as follows: **N1:** 2 sts; **N2:** 4 sts; **N3:** 4 sts.
With N1, pick up and knit 2 sts in the st CO at underarm—12 sts on needles.
Place a locking st marker into the first st for BOR.
Next rnd: Knit.

Cont in St st until sleeve meas 1½" [4 cm] from underarm.

For a garter stitch cuff *(shown in pullover 1):*
Next rnd: Purl.
Cont in garter st for 2 more rnds.
Next rnd: Bind off loosely knitwise.

For a ribbed cuff *(shown in pullover 2):*
Next rnd: *K1, p1; rep from * to end.
Cont in rib for 1 more rnd.
Next rnd: Bind off loosely knitwise.

Finishing
Weave in ends. Steam- or wet-block ornament to finished measurements.

Embroider snowflake *(shown in pullover 1):*
With accent yarn, beg at center front of pullover, and in back stitch, using 1" [2.5 cm] for largest sts and ¼" [.5 cm] for smallest sts, embroider each section of the snowflake from the center out.

Cardigan

Using the long-tail cast on, CO 16 sts. Do not join. Work back and forth on 2 double-pointed needles (dpns).

Begin neck trim

First row: (RS) Knit.

Next row *place markers:* K4, place marker (pm), k2, pm, k4, pm, k2, pm, k4 sts to end.

Begin raglan shaping

Next row *inc row:* (RS) *Knit to 1 st before marker (m), k1-f/b, slip marker (sl m), k1-f/b; rep from * three more times, knit to end (8 sts inc'd)—24 sts.

Next row: K2, purl to last 2 sts, k2.

Rep *inc row* every RS row three more times—48 sts on needles; 8 sts for each front, 10 sts for each sleeve, and 12 sts for back.

Next row: K2, purl to last 2 sts, k2.

Separate body and sleeves

Next row: (RS) Knit across front sts to m, remove m, place sts for sleeve onto waste yarn, remove m, using the backward loop cast on, CO 1 st, knit across back sts to m, remove m, place sts for sleeve onto waste yarn, remove m, CO 1 st, knit to end—30 sts on needles.

Next row: K2, purl to last 2 sts, k2.

For a solid-colored body *(shown in cardigan 1):*

Next row: (RS) Knit.

Next row: K2, purl to last 2 sts, k2.

Cont as est until body meas 1½" [4 cm] from underarm, ending after a WS row. Proceed to 1x1 or 2x2 rib trim.

For a striped body *(shown in cardigan 2):*

Next row: (RS) With CC, knit.

Next row: With CC, k2, purl to last 2 sts, k2.

Next row: With MC, knit.

Next row: With MC, k2, purl to last 2 sts, k2.

Cont as est until body meas 1½" [4 cm] from underarm, ending after a WS row. Proceed to 1x1 or 2x2 rib trim.

For 1x1 rib trim *(shown in cardigan 2):*

Next row: (RS) *K1, p1; rep from * to end.

Cont in rib for 1 more row.

Next row: (RS) Bind off loosely in pattern.

For 2x2 rib trim *(shown in cardigan 1):*

Next row: (RS) *K2, p2; rep from * to last 2 sts, k2.

Next row: *P2, k2; rep from * to last 2 sts, p2.

Next row: Bind off loosely in pattern.

Sleeves

Arrange sts for sleeve onto 3 dpns as follows:

N1: 2 sts; N2: 4 sts; N3: 4 sts.

With N1, pick up and knit 2 sts in the st CO at underarm—12 sts on needles. Place a locking st marker into the first st for BOR.

Next rnd: Knit.

Cont in St st until sleeve meas 1½" [4 cm] from underarm.

For 1x1 rib cuff *(shown in cardigan 2):*
Next rnd: *K1, p1; rep from * to end.
Cont in rib for 1 more rnd.
Next rnd: Bind off loosely in pattern.

For 2x2 rib cuff *(shown in cardigan 1):*
Next rnd: *K2, p2; rep from * to end.
Cont in rib for 1 more rnd.
Next rnd: Bind off loosely in pattern.

Finishing

Weave in ends. Steam- or wet-block ornament to finished measurements.

To make an ornament loop:

Cut an 8" [20 cm] length of accent yarn. Using a tapestry needle, draw yarn through a CO st at center of neck edge or top of one sleeve and fold in half so that yarn is doubled. Use an overhand knot to close loop at desired length and trim ends.

For a button closure:

Overlap garter stitch fronts. Arrange buttons however you like: one or two just below the neck edge (as shown) or evenly spaced down the front band. Sew buttons on through both layers of fabric.

For a tie closure:

Cut a 6" [15 cm] length of accent yarn. Using a tapestry needle, draw yarn through edge stitches on each front, close to neck edge. Tie into a small bow and trim ends.

Not sure what size sweater to make for your little one? If you have a tee shirt that fits her, you can take the guesswork out of your project. All you need is a basic tee that fits the intended wearer. By using measurements taken from the tee and following the steps below, you can easily knit up a top-down raglan cardigan with a classic 2x2 rib trim. If the tee fits the wearer, so will your sweater!

Step 1: Knit a gauge swatch

As always, start with a good swatch. With the yarn you've chosen for your sweater, and using the recommended needle (check your yarn label), cast on and knit up a 6" [15 cm] square. (Use the gauge numbers shown on the label to guestimate the number of stitches to cast on. For example, at 4 stitches per inch, cast on 24 stitches for a 6" swatch.)

Then block your swatch and notice how it feels.

- Too stiff and tight? Try a larger needle.
- Too loose and floppy? Try a smaller needle.
- Swatch just right? Carry on…

What you'll need:

- Worksheets (pages 49-52)
- Tee shirt to fit intended recipient
- Two straight rulers, at least 12" [30.5 cm] long, or one ruler and one tape measure
- Yarn and needles appropriate for project (circular and double-pointed needles)
- Calculator
- Stitch markers
- Waste yarn
- Tapestry needle
- Buttons appropriate to project
- Sewing needle, matching thread

too tight…

too loose…

just right!

Same yarn, same number of stitches: Changing needle size creates different fabrics in feel and finished measurements.

Measure a 4" [10 cm] square in the center of your swatch. Count the number of stitches across this section. Then count the number of rows in 4" [10 cm]. Finally, round each to a whole number, then divide by 4 [10] to get your stitch and row gauge. Enter these numbers into your worksheet (page 49).

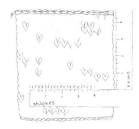

Step 2: Measure your tee

Use a tee shirt that fits your cardigan's recipient, preferably one with a little ease. If making a long sleeve cardigan, use a long sleeve tee. Lay the tee flat and with a straight ruler, take measurements as follows for your worksheet:

Note: Round your measurements to ¼" [.5 cm] for neater calculations.

1: neck width
Work the curved edge of the neck into a more straight line for this measurement (see note below).

2: chest width
Measure flat, straight across chest, just below the underarm.

3: yoke depth
Measure flat, straight down from center of back neck.

5: top of sleeve width
Measure straight across sleeve just below underarm.

7: cuff width
Measure straight across, just like top of sleeve.

6: sleeve length
With the ruler still across sleeve at underarm, measure straight down from the underarm to the end of the cuff.

4: body length
Measure straight down to the bottom edge of the tee.

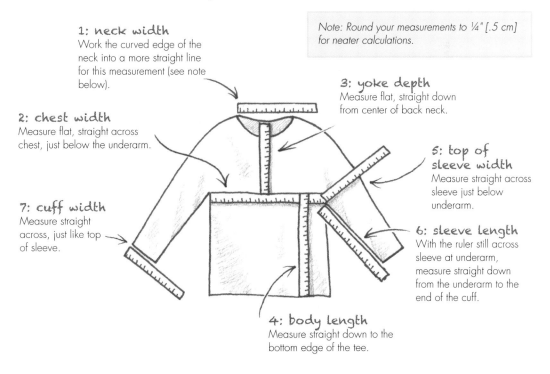

Note: To measure neck width, don't stretch; just gently coax the edge straight and line one edge up with the end of the ruler to measure.

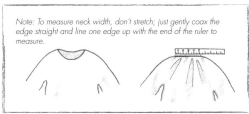

Step 3: Fill in Calculation A--and start knitting!

On the worksheet fill in the numbers for *Calculation A* (page 49) to figure out how many stitches to cast on for the neck edge. *Calculation A* takes your neck measurement and converts it to stitches for back neck (b), sleeve tops (c), and fronts.

Cast on your stitches

With circular needle (circ) and using the long-tail cast on, CO 1 st for front, place marker (pm), CO sleeve sts (c), pm, CO back sts (b), pm, CO sleeve sts (c), pm, CO 1 st for front.

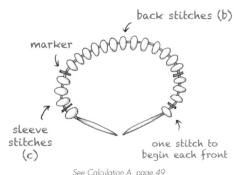

back stitches (b)

marker

sleeve stitches (c)

one stitch to begin each front

See Calculation A, page 49

Step 4: Begin raglan increases

Note: For more information on raglan yoke and neck shaping, see the Basic Cardigan, page 10.

First row: (RS) K1-f/b, slip marker (sl m), *k1-f/b, knit to 1 st before next marker (m), k1-f/b, sl m; rep from * two more times, k1-f/b in last st (8 sts inc'd).
Next row: (WS) Purl.

Step 5: Continue raglan increases and Begin front neck shaping

Next row: (RS) (K1-f/b) two times, sl m, *k1-f/b, knit to 1 st before m, k1-f/b, sl m; rep from * two more times, (k1-f/b) two times (10 sts inc'd).
Next row: (WS) Purl.
Next row *neck and raglan inc row:* (RS) *K1-f/b, knit to 1 st before m, k1-f/b, sl m; rep from * three more times, k1-f/b, knit to last st, k1-f/b (10 sts inc'd).

Rep *neck and raglan inc row* every RS row until yoke measures the depth noted for your size on the neck depth chart, next page. End after a WS row.

Slip your stitches from the needle onto waste yarn for measuring front widths. If the edges roll, give them a light steam to straighten. There should be a 1" [2.5 cm] gap between fronts for button band. If your gap is wider, use *Calculation B* (page 50) to determine how many front stitches to cast on.
If your front gap is just right at 1" [2.5 cm], cast on 1 stitch at each neck edge.

Front neck cast on row: With WS still facing, using the backward loop cast on, CO 1 st (or d from *Calculation B*), turn work, *knit to 1 st before m, k1-f/b, sl m, k1-f/b; rep from * three more times, knit to end, then using the backward loop cast on, CO same number of sts as for first front.

Neck depth based on tee size
- For sizes under 4, work to 1" [2.5 cm].
- For sizes 4-8, work to 1½" [4 cm].
- For sizes 8-12, work to 2" [5 cm].

At this point, you've finished shaping the neck. From here you'll only increase stitches at the four raglan lines.

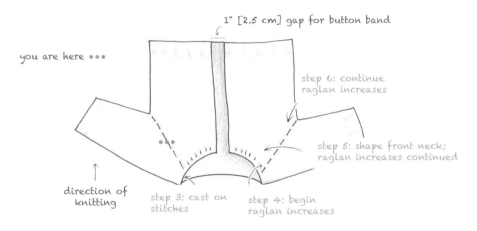

1" [2.5 cm] gap for button band

you are here ●●●

step 6: continue raglan increases

step 5: shape front neck; raglan increases continued

direction of knitting

step 3: cast on stitches

step 4: begin raglan increases

steps 3-6: from cast on through raglan shaping

Step 6: Continue raglan increases

Next row *raglan inc row:* (RS) *Knit to 1 st before m, k1-f/b, sl m, k1-f/b; rep from * three more times, knit to end (8 sts inc'd).

Rep *raglan inc row* every RS row until yoke measures approx 2" [5 cm] less than your desired yoke depth (Measurement 3, page 49).

Now it's time to check your sweater measurements and compare them to the target numbers on your worksheet. Slip your stitches onto waste yarn again. If edges roll too much, steam lightly to straighten. Lay the sweater on a flat surface with the back facing up, and measure across the back, from one raglan marker to the other. Then measure along the sleeve in the same manner, from the raglan marker to where the sleeve folds toward the front of the piece.

- If you've arrived at the targeted chest and sleeve widths (Measurements 2 and 5, page 49), simply knit even (without increasing) until you've reached your yoke depth.
- If your sleeves are the right width, but the body is too narrow, work *Calculation C* (page 50) to determine how many more increases to work on fronts and back (see *body only inc row*, below.)
- If your body is the right width, but the sleeves are too narrow, work *Calculation D* (page 50) to determine how many more increases to work on the sleeves (see *sleeve only inc row*, below.)
- If both body and sleeves are too narrow, use *Calculations C & D* together to determine how many more *raglan inc rows* to work.

To work body-only or sleeve-only increase rows:

Sleeve-only inc row: (RS) *Knit to m, sl m, k1-f/b, knit to 1 st before m, k1-f/b, sl m; rep from * one more time, knit to end (4 sts inc'd in sleeves only).

Body-only inc row: (RS) *Knit to 1 st before m, k1-f/b, sl m, knit to next m, sl m, k1-f/b; rep from * one more time, knit to end (4 sts inc'd in body only).

Continue working in stockinette and making increases as needed until you reach the proper yoke depth (Measurement 3, page 49), ending after a WS row.

- If you work all your increases before you hit your yoke depth, work even (no increases).
- If you reach the yoke depth before you've worked all the increases, no problem. Use *Calculation E* (page 50) to determine how many extra underarm stitches to cast on in Step 7.

Step 7: Separate body and sleeves

Underarm cast on row: (RS) Knit across front sts to m, remove m, place sts to next m onto waste yarn for sleeve, remove m, using the backward loop cast on, CO 1 st (or e from *Calculation E*), knit across back sts to next m, remove m, place sts to next m onto waste yarn for sleeve, remove m, using the backward loop cast on, CO 1 st (or e from *Calculation E*), knit across front sts to end.

Now only stitches for the body of your cardigan are on the needles. Sleeve stitches are held for later.

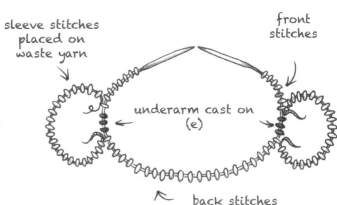

sleeve stitches placed on waste yarn

front stitches

underarm cast on (e)

back stitches

Step 8: Work body

This is the easy part! Work in stockinette to the length you like, less 1-2" [2.5-5 cm] for trim. Just before your last RS row, take a stitch count. For a symmetric 2x2 rib trim, stitches must be a mulitple of 4 + 2. Use *Calculation F* (page 51) to determine if you have to increase or decrease a stitch or two for a balanced rib.

Begin trim

Next row: (WS) *P2, k2; rep from * to last 2 sts, p2.

Next row: (RS) *K2, p2; rep from * to last 2 sts, k2.

Rep these 2 rows to desired length.

Next row: Bind off loosely in pattern.

For a balanced rib:

To decrease 1 st: Knit to center of sts, k2tog, knit to end.

To decrease 2 sts: K1, k2tog, knit to last 3 sts, ssk, k1.

To increase 1 st: Knit to center of sts, m1, knit to end.

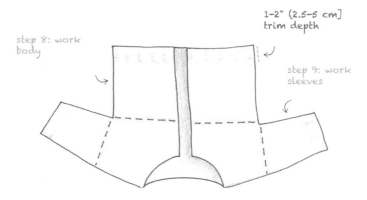

1-2" (2.5-5 cm)
trim depth

step 8: work
body

step 9: work
sleeves

steps 8 and 9: work body and sleeves

Step 9: Work sleeves

Place sts held for one sleeve onto double-pointed needles. Pick up and knit 1 st in each st cast on for underarm until you reach center of underarm, pm for beg of rnd, then pick up 1 st in each rem underarm CO st (if you only cast on 1 st at underarm, place the marker just after it).

First rnd: Knit to end.

For a short sleeve, skip to cuff trim now, or work in stockinette for up to 1" [2.5 cm], then begin your trim.

For a long sleeve, use *Calculation G* (page 51) to work out your sleeve shaping.

Begin sleeve shaping

Work in stockinette stitch for _____ (i) rnds.

Next rnd *dec rnd:* K1, k2tog, knit to last 3 sts, ssk, k1 (2 sts dec'd).

Rep *dec rnd* every _____ (i) rnds _____ (g) times.

Measure the length of your sleeve and if necessary, work even until it's 1-2" [2.5-5 cm] short of your target length.

For a symmetric 2x2 rib trim, stitches must be a multiple of 4. If needed, use *Calculation H* (page 52) to determine stitch adjustment, then increase or decrease as described on page 45.

Begin cuff trim

Next rnd: *K2, p2; rep from * to end.

Rep this rnd every rnd to desired length.

Next rnd: Bind off loosely in pattern.

Step 10: Finishing

Weave in ends. Steam- or wet-block cardigan to finished measurements.

Neck band

For great illustrated tutorials on picking up stitches, visit our blog: quinceandco.com.
With RS facing and circ, beg at right front neck edge (CO at front neck), pick up and knit along neck edge as follows: 1 st in each CO st for front neck, 1 st for every 2 rows along each front neck edge, and 1 st in each CO st and 1 st in each raglan line along shoulders and back neck.

For a symmetric 2x2 rib trim, stitches must be a multiple of 4. If necessary, use *Calculation I* (page 52) to determine how many sts to increase or decrease in your first row.

> For a balanced rib, on your first row (WS):
>
> **To decrease 1 st:** P3, k1, k2tog, *p2, k2; rep from * to last 3 sts, p3.
>
> **To decrease 2 sts:** P3, k1, k2tog, *p2, k2; rep from * to last 6 sts, p2, ssk, k1, p3.
>
> **To increase 1 st:** P3, k1, m1, *p2, k2; rep from * to last 2 sts, p3.
>
> **To begin rib with no adjustment:** P3, *k2, p2; rep from * to last st, p1.

Next row: (RS) K3, *p2, k2; rep from * to last st, k1.
Next row: P3, *k2, p2; rep from * to last st, p1.
Cont in rib for 1" [2.5 cm].
Next row: Bind off in pattern.

Button band

Use *Calculation J* to determine proper pick-up rate for your gauge. With RS facing and circ, beg at neck edge of left front, pick up and knit sts to bottom edge at the rate given for your gauge. Stitches must be a multiple of 4 + 2.
See *Basic Cardigan* (page 14) if you need to adjust your pick-up stitch count.

Begin rib

Next row: (WS) *P2, k2; rep from * to last 2 sts, p2.
Next row: (RS) *K2, p2; rep from * to last 2 sts, k2.
Cont in rib for 1" [2.5 cm]. Make note of how many rows you worked.
Next row: Bind off in pattern.

Buttonhole band

With RS facing and circ, beg at lower edge of right front, pick up and knit same number of sts along right front to neck edge as you did for left front.

Begin rib

First row: (WS) *P2, k2; rep from * to last 2 sts, p2.
Next row: *K2, p2; rep from * to last 2 sts, k2.
Cont in rib for about half the rows you worked for button band (including the 2 rows already worked), ending after a RS row. If total rows is an odd number, round down.

Buttonhole placement

With WS facing, place a locking st marker 2 sts away from neck edge, then place markers for buttonholes as you like, being sure the number of stitches between markers is always a multiple of 4.

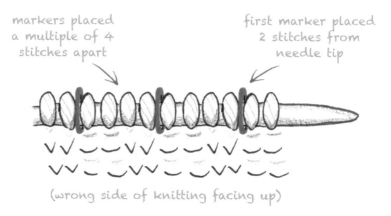

markers placed a multiple of 4 stitches apart

first marker placed 2 stitches from needle tip

(wrong side of knitting facing up)

Next row *buttonhole row:* P2, remove m, yo, k2tog, *work in rib to next m, remove m, yo, k2tog; rep from * for each marker, work in rib to end.
Cont in rib until same number of rows have been worked as for button band.
Next row: Bind off in pattern.

Sew buttons opposite buttonholes.
Weave in remaining ends and block again, if you like.

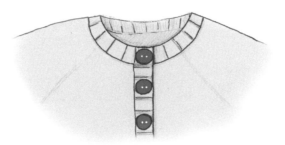

Cardigan Worksheet

Measurements

For: _____

Tee size: _____

Yarn: _____

Needle size: _____

_____ stitch gauge

_____ row gauge

1. Neck _____

2. Chest _____

3. Yoke depth _____

4. Body length _____

5. Top of sleeve _____

6. Sleeve length _____

7. Cuff _____

....

Calculation A: Cast on stitches (Step 3, page 42)

_____ + 2 [5] = _____ x _____ = _____

| neck
width
(1) | " [cm]
to be
filled by
neck band | neck
" [cm]
before
trim | stitch
gauge | sts for
back half
of neck *
(a) | * round to
a multiple
of 4 |

back stitches: _____ ÷ 4 = _____ x 3 = _____

rounded sts · · · sts · · · back
for back half · · · · · · · · cast on sts
of neck (a) · · · · · · · · · · (b)

sleeve stitches: _____ ÷ 4 = _____

rounded sts · · · cast on sts
for back half · · for one sleeve
of neck (a) · · · · · · (c)

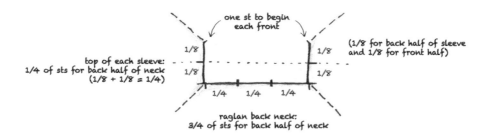

one st to begin
each front

top of each sleeve:
1/4 of sts for back half of neck
(1/8 + 1/8 = 1/4)

1/8   1/8

1/8   1/8

1/4   1/4   1/4

(1/8 for back half of sleeve
and 1/8 for front half)

raglan back neck:
3/4 of sts for back half of neck

Calculation B: Neck shaping (Step 5, page 42)

_____ − 1 [2.5] = _____ × _____ = _____ ÷ 2 = _____

| " [cm] of gap between fronts | " [cm] for button band | " [cm] needed to be increased | stitch gauge | sts to be increased * | | cast on for each front (d) |

* round to an even number

If front gap is already 1" [2.5 cm] cast on 1 st at each front.

....

Calulations C & D are only needed if body or sleeves are too narrow.

Calculation C: Body-only increases (Step 6, page 44)

_____ − _____ = _____ × _____ = _____ ÷ 2 = _____

| chest width (2) | current chest width | " [cm] needed to be increased | stitch gauge | sts to be increased * | | body-only inc rows needed |

* round to an even number

....

Calculation D: Sleeve-only increases (Step 6, page 44)

_____ − _____ = _____ × _____ = _____ ÷ 2 = _____

| top of sleeve width (5) | current sleeve width | " [cm] needed to be increased | stitch gauge | sts to be increased * | | sleeve-only inc rows needed |

* round to an even number

If both calulations are needed, work raglan inc row for the smaller number, then work the remaining increases needed for the larger number of the two (either body-only or sleeve-only).

....

Calculation E is only needed if you still have more increases to go while your yoke depth is just right.

Calculation E: Underarm cast on (Step 6, page 44)

_____ × 2 = _____

| # of increases still needed to be worked * ⟶ | cast on for each underarm (e) |

* If casting on stitches to achieve chest width makes the sleeves a little too wide, no problem! A bit more room in a sleeve is better than too snug.

Calculation F: Body rib adjustment (Step 8, page 45)

_____ − 2 = _____ ÷ 4 = _____   * If this is a whole number,
sts on   sts   repeats in   begin your ribbing with no
needles   2X2 rib *   adjustment; if this is a
                                           decimal, round DOWN to
                                         the nearest whole number.

_____ × 4 = _____ + 2 = _____
rib repeats   sts   ideal
rounded   stitch count
DOWN

_____ − _____ = _____   * This will either be 1, 2, or 3 sts.
sts on   ideal   stitches   If it's 3, increase 1 st instead.
needles   stitch   to
        count   decrease *

Calculation G: Sleeve shaping (Step 9, page 46)

_____ × _____ = _____   * If top of sleeve stitch count is
cuff   stitch   sts needed   an even number, round to even,
(7)   gauge   at cuff *   if it's an odd number,
                 (f)   round to odd.

_____ − _____ = _____ ÷ 2 = _____ − 1 = _____
sts on   rounded   sts to   total   first   dec rows
needles   cuff sts   decrease   decreases   dec   to go
         (f)   needed   row   (g)

_____ − _____ = _____ × _____ = _____
sleeve   " [cm]   " [cm] to   row   rows to
length   cuff   decrease   gauge   decrease
(6)   trim   in   in (h)

_____ ÷ _____ = _____   * round DOWN to a whole number;
rows to   dec rows   decrease   you will work this number of rows
decrease   to go   rate *   before your first decrease, then
in (h)   (g)   (i)   keep decreasing at this rate until
                                     you reach your target cuff stitches.

Calculation H: Sleeve rib adjustment (Step 9, page 46)

_____ ÷ 4 = _____ × 4 = _____   * If this is a whole number,
sts on   repeats in   ideal stitch   begin your ribbing with no
needles   2X2 rib * ⟶   count   adjustment; if this is a
                                        decimal, round DOWN to
                                        the nearest whole number.

_____ - _____ = _____
sts on   ideal   stitches   * This will either be 1, 2, or 3 sts.
needles stitch   to   If it's 3, increase 1 st instead.
       count   decrease *

Calculation I: Neck rib adjustment (Step 10, page 47)

_____ ÷ 4 = _____ × 4 = _____   * If this is a whole number,
sts on   repeats in   ideal stitch   begin your ribbing with no
needles   2X2 rib * ⟶   count   adjustment; if this is a
                                        decimal, round DOWN to
                                        the nearest whole number.

_____ - _____ = _____
sts on   ideal   stitches   * This will either be 1, 2, or 3 sts.
needles stitch   to   If it's 3, increase 1 st instead.
       count   decrease *

Calculation J: Pick-up rate for your gauge

_____ ÷ _____ = _____
stitch   row   pick-up   * This number will be less than 1.
gauge   gauge   rate *   It will be a decimal.
                         Find the number closest in
                         the rate key below.

Rate Key:

if your rate is nearest:	pick up:	for every:
0.66	2 sts	3 rows
0.75	3 sts	4 rows
0.85	4 sts	5 rows

Standard abbreviations

approx	approximately	m	marker(s)
beg	begin(ning); begin(s)	p	purl
BO	bind off	patt(s)	pattern(s)
BOR	beginning of round	pc(s)	piece(s)
CO	cast on	pm	place marker
CC	contrasting color	rem	remain(ing); remain(s)
circ	circular needle	rep	repeat(ing); repeat(s)
cm	centimeter(s)	RH	right hand
cont	continue(s); continuing	rib	ribbing
dec('d)	decrease(d)	rnd(s)	round(s)
dpn(s)	double-pointed needle(s)	RS	right side
est	establish(ed)	sl	slip
g	gram(s)	sl m	slip marker
inc('d)	increase(d)	st(s)	stitch(es)
k	knit	St st	stockinette stitch
LH	left hand	tog	together
MC	main color	WS	wrong side
meas	measures	yd	yard(s)
mm	millimeter(s)		

Special abbreviations

k1-f/b (knit 1, front and back): Knit into the front loop, then the back loop of next stitch (1 stitch increased).

k2tog: Knit 2 stitches together (1 stitch decreased, leans to the right).

k3tog: Knit 3 stitches together (2 stitches decreased, leans to the right).

m1 (make 1): Insert LH needle from front to back under horizontal strand between stitch just worked and next stitch, knit lifted strand through the back loop (1 stitch increased).

M1R (make 1 right slanting): Insert LH needle from back to front under horizontal strand between stitch just worked and next stitch, knit lifted strand through the front loop (1 stitch increased).

M1L (make 1 left slanting): Insert LH needle from front to back under horizontal strand between stitch just worked and next stitch, knit lifted strand through the back loop (1 stitch increased).

p2tog: Purl 2 stitches together (1 stitch decreased).

skp: Slip 1 stitch purlwise to RH needle, k1, pass slipped stitch over (1 stitch decreased).

ssk (slip, slip, knit): Slip 2 stitches one at a time knitwise to the RH needle; return stitches to LH needle in turned position and knit them together through the back loops (1 stitch decreased, leans to the left).

yo (yarn over): Bring yarn between needles to the front, then over RH needle ready to knit the next stitch (1 stitch increased).

for crochet

ch (chain): Wrap the yarn around the crochet hook (yarn over) and draw it through the loop on the hook to form the first chain. Rep this step as many times as instructed. (The loop on the hook is never included when counting the number of chains.)

sl stitch (slip stitch): Insert crochet hook in the indicated stitch, yarn over and draw through both the stitch and the loop on the hook.

Basic math terms

whole number: A number without fractions or decimals.

positive number: A number that is greater than zero.

even number: A number that when divided by two, produces a whole number.

odd number: A number that when divided by two, does not produce a whole number.

Techniques

Basic stitch patterns
Stockinette stitch (St st)
Worked flat
Knit on the RS, purl on the WS.
In the round
Knit every round.

Garter stitch
Worked flat
Knit every row.
In the round
Rnd 1: Knit.
Rnd 2: Purl.
Repeat Rnds 1 and 2.

Helpful links
For help with the following techniques, visit our blog:
long-tail cast on
backward loop cast on
picking up stitches

For instructions on **embroidering the back stitch**, see:
www.sublimestitching.com/pages/how-to-back-stitch
For instructions on **grafting (Kitchener stitch)**, we like:
www.knitty.com/ISSUEsummer04/FEATtheresasum04.html
For instructions on the **three-needle bind off**, try:
www.knitty.com/ISSUEfall06/FEATfall06TT.html
For further help with **making an i-cord**, try:
www.techknitting.blogspot.com/2007/02/how-to-make-i-cord.html

Susan B. Anderson lives and knits in Madison, Wisconsin. She has authored six knitting books, including the best-selling *Itty-Bitty Hats*, *Itty-Bitty Nursery*, *Itty-Bitty Toys* series, *Topsy-Turvy Inside-Out*, and *Kids' Knitting Workshop*. Susan has four popular Craftsy.com online workshops and has published designs in magazines such as *Making*, *Taproot*, *Parents*, *Interweave Knits*, *Noro*, and *Knit Simple*. With Quince & Co, Susan has published several well-received knitted toy collections: *Mary, Millie & Morgan*, *Ben & Buddy*, and *String Along Toys*. For over 10 years Susan has written her award-winning blog, susanbanderson.blogspot.com. Susan's favorite part of her knitting career is getting to travel across the United States and beyond to teach and meet knitters from all over the world.

Quince & Company makes beautiful yarns in natural fibers. We spin our yarns primarily in New England from wool sourced from American sheep. We began with four classic wool yarns in weights from sport to chunky. Today we make twelve different yarns in the US and import two organic linen yarns from Italy. We ship our yarns all over the world—from Tanzania to Korea to Argentina. Find out more about us at quinceandco.com.

Contributors

Editor / Pam Allen
Technical Editor & Project Coordinator / Jerusha Robinson
Technical Editor & Worksheet Design / Dawn Catanzaro
Layout & Technical Illustrations / Leila Raabe
Other Illustrations / Susan B. Anderson
Photography / Whitney Hayward
Copy Editing / Victoria Fura & Bristol Ivy